YOUR KNOWLEDGE HAS VALUE

- We will publish your bachelor's and master's thesis, essays and papers

- Your own eBook and book - sold worldwide in all relevant shops

- Earn money with each sale

Upload your text at www.GRIN.com
and publish for free

Bibliographic information published by the German National Library:

The German National Library lists this publication in the National Bibliography; detailed bibliographic data are available on the Internet at http://dnb.dnb.de .

This book is copyright material and must not be copied, reproduced, transferred, distributed, leased, licensed or publicly performed or used in any way except as specifically permitted in writing by the publishers, as allowed under the terms and conditions under which it was purchased or as strictly permitted by applicable copyright law. Any unauthorized distribution or use of this text may be a direct infringement of the author s and publisher s rights and those responsible may be liable in law accordingly.

Imprint:

Copyright © 2015 GRIN Verlag, Open Publishing GmbH
Print and binding: Books on Demand GmbH, Norderstedt Germany
ISBN: 9783668547438

This book at GRIN:

http://www.grin.com/en/e-book/376961/the-acceptance-of-capital-punishment-a-comparison-of-ernest-j-gaine-s

Natascha Niedner

The Acceptance of Capital Punishment. A Comparison of Ernest J. Gaine's Novel "A Lesson Before Dying" and Today's Views

GRIN Publishing

GRIN - Your knowledge has value

Since its foundation in 1998, GRIN has specialized in publishing academic texts by students, college teachers and other academics as e-book and printed book. The website www.grin.com is an ideal platform for presenting term papers, final papers, scientific essays, dissertations and specialist books.

Visit us on the internet:

http://www.grin.com/

http://www.facebook.com/grincom

http://www.twitter.com/grin_com

List of Contents

1. Introduction...2

2. History...3
   2.1. The development of the death penalty..3

3. Novel "A Lesson Before Dying"...5
   3.1. Summary...5

4. Challenges of African-American citizen...6
   4.1. Racism..7
   4.2. Poverty...9

5. Comparison of the novel and reality..10

6. Survey results..11

7. Conclusion...12

8. List of references 14

9. Appendix..15

1. Introduction

> "Far from being unanimous in their support for the death penalty, Americans are deeply divided over the humanity, wisdom and efficacy of capital punishment."[1]

This quotation by Simon Wendt should inspire to think about the subject of capital punishment and its purpose in the United States society. The history of violence goes along with the history of human kind[2] and the Criminal Justice System maintained a race-based hierarchy for centuries with many citizens still thinking lowly of humans with a different color of skin. By discussing the novel "A Lesson Before Dying" by Ernest J. Gaines I would like to approach the question to what extent capital punishment is accepted in the universe of the novel in comparison to the modern time in the United States. I chose the subject of capital punishment because I have long been interested in it due to the fact that I think that capital punishment is an inhuman, irrevocable punishment. When several books of American literature were presented to our class I wanted to incorporate my interest of the subject directly in my term paper. The novel "A Lesson Before Dying" therefore was my first choice because it addresses the predicament of African-American citizen who strive for dignity in a universe that often denies it.

After I found the main question for this term paper I started to focus my research by concentrating on how exactly capital punishment was introduced to the American society and how it modified in time. In this context I will give a brief overview on the history of capital punishment in the United States as an introduction and give a short summary of the book to classify it in the modern time and the late 1940s. With that foreknowledge, I will take a closer look at the challenges of African-American citizen due to their conviction in a time of racial segregation, for I aim to show the problems of the U.S. American Criminal Justice System in the novel compared to today. Then follows a comparison of

---

[1] Manfred Berg, Stefan Kapsch, Franz Streng, *"Criminal Justice in the United States and Germany"*, Universitätsverlag WINTER Heidelberg, 2006, p.65
[2] Frank Müller, *"Streitfall Todesstrafe"*, Patmos Verlag Düsseldorf 1998, p.7ff

the situation in the novel with reality because I thereby want to demonstrate how much the United States society has changed regarding to the acceptance of capital punishment. To underline my conclusion, which will be the last part of my term paper, I created a survey of which results will be analyzed and evaluated. At the end I am going to close my question with a prospect for better times of African-American citizen in the future.

2. History
2.1. The development of the death penalty

The history of capital punishment in the United States of America goes back to the beginning of the 17th century. At the time of the colonial settlement in the USA, the British colonial rulers brought this new aspect of punishment from their old native country, where they had carried out executions for centuries even for minor offenses[3]. In 1608, the British Captain George Kendall was executed in Virginia because he had been spying for Spain. He became the first victim of capital punishment on American ground. Capital punishment in the U.S. was first put into question during the 18th century by philosophers like Beccaria, Voltaire or Montesquieu, who were against capital punishment.

The State of Pennsylvania was one of the forerunners of the relaxation of the capital punishment: In 1794, only those people were condemned to death who had killed someone (also called "first degree murder"). After this first step, many other federal states reduced the number of possible crimes which were to be punished with death. Furthermore, capital punishment was always applied as a sort of deterrence from committing heavy criminal offenses. Beginning in the 19th century, demands for an abolition of capital punishment spread across the whole country. Since 1834 the executions have only been carried out behind prison walls[4]. In 1853 the federal states of the south however almost nothing changed. The South even applied sharper laws for slaves who had to

---
[3] Jürgen Martschukat, "*Die Geschichte der Todesstrafe in Nordamerika – Von der Kolonialzeit bis zur Gegenwart*", Verlag C.H.Beck oHG, München 2002, p.13
[4] Die Geschichte der Todesstrafe in Nordamerika – Von der Kolonialzeit bis zur Gegenwart, p.51

fear a more severe punishment and were sentenced to death for minor offenses than white people. Also did they hardly ever experience a fair process.

The support for the abolition of capital punishment decreased (in the USA) during the American civil war in the 1860s. Death penalty was modernized with the help of Thomas Edison, who created the electric chair[5]. He presented it for the first time in New York in 1888 and from then on it was used by many federal states, because it seemed more human. Nevertheless, during the first 17 years of the 20th century, six other federal states abandoned the death penalty because of the abolitionists[6]. However, that was only one short-term episode because up to 1920, five of these six federal states had reintroduced capital punishment. This was above all the expression of growing social tensions and duo to the fear of a socialist revolution in the United States. In 1924, Nevada was the first federal state in which executions were carried out by deadly gas supplied in a specially established chamber. At that time, was also seen as a farther step to a more human death penalty. During the following years in which the USA suffered from the worldwide economic crisis, the number of executions clearly increased and reached a climax in the 1930th by an average of 167 executions per year.

After the Second World War and the United Nations signing "The Universal Declaration of Human Rights" in 1948, the number of imposed death-penalties decreased because "Everyone has the right to life, liberty and security of person."[7]. Many other nations abolished the capital punishment completely and also in the United States of America the number of it's advocates sank. If there were 1300 executions in the USA from 1940 to 1949, there were only 191 criminals who were executed from 1960 to 1976. This reflects the changed public opinion on the subject at the time which also expressed itself in the fact that the Supreme Court of the USA repeatedly dealt with the question of the legality of the capital punishment. The enforcement of death sentences was actually put on ice due to this juridical insecurity in 1968.

---

5   Death Penalty Information Center - Nineteenth Century, URL:
    http://www.deathpenaltyinfo.org/part-i-history-death-penalty#intro [02.03.2015 ; 19:11]
6   The abolitionists were against capital punishment
7   The Universal Declaration of Human Rights, Article 3, The United Nations 1948, URL:
    http://www.un.org/en/documents/udhr/ [18.03.2015 ; 13:55]

Finally, in June 1972, the Supreme Court came to the decision that the procedure with which criminals were executed in Georgia did not fulfill to the constitution of the American state. With this decision, the uppermost court forbade the capital punishment in 40 federal states, because they used the same procedures as Georgia[8]. The laws were written anew as a result of the federal states being checked in 1976 by the Supreme Court once more and were confirmed in the same year - the States indicated in the legal texts from that date directives by which aggravating or facilitating circumstances must be assessed in the act in question. At the same time, the court confirmed the constitutional moderation of capital punishment itself. In January 1977, the first death sentence since 1968 was executed in Utah.

While the applicability of capital punishment was confirmed by the highest American court, the jurisdiction nevertheless dealt with the hardest form of the punishment also during the following years. Besides, the Supreme Court has given stricter regulations for the crimes which can be punished with death at all. In 1994, President Bill Clinton extended the list of the crimes to be avenged with death to various circumstances for murder. However, treason and drug trafficking were also enclosed in that list. Under the impression of the bomb attack in Oklahoma City, Clinton provided criminals who were sentenced to death for a shortening of the appeal possibilities in 1996. In 2007, the federal state of New Jersey stroked capital punishment from its laws, followed by New Mexico in 2009 and Illinois in 2011. At the same time, the approval of capital punishment has reached a new low in the whole population in the United States.

3. Novel "A Lesson Before Dying"
3.1. Summary

Set in the fictional town of Bayonne, Louisiana, the narrator Grant Wiggins tells the story of Jefferson, a 21-year-old man, who is wrongfully accused and

---

[8] Die Geschichte der Todesstrafe in Nordamerika – Von der Kolonialzeit bis zur Gegenwart, p.130

convicted of the robbery and murder of Alcee Gropé, a white storekeeper, and is sentenced to death by electrocution.

At his trial, Jefferson's court-appointed lawyer argues that two of his acquaintances were to blame for the charges and that the evidence seems to corroborate this. Jefferson's lawyer also points out that sentencing him to death would be like killing a hog in the electric chair, for he would lack the intelligence to plan a robbery and commit the murder, just like an animal. Nevertheless, Jefferson is convicted and sentenced to death by the all-white jury. His godmother, Miss Emma, is determined that Jefferson will not die like a hog but as a man and turns to Grant Wiggins, a black teacher at the local plantation school, and asks him to visit Jefferson in prison to educate him, hoping that he will die with dignity.

Grant agrees reluctantly to visit Jefferson over the next month until the day of his execution. Grant's initial efforts of teaching Jefferson are disappointing. He has accepted his lawyer's depiction of him as a hog, is almost catatonic and unwilling to communicate. With patience, Grant tries to make him belief that his lawyer's conception of him as a subhuman is wrong and that others care about him as a human. Jefferson slowly begins to open up to Grant and accepts a small portable radio from him which he takes as a kind, caring gift. Then Grant encourages him to write down everything he feels and thinks about and in the end Jefferson admits that he is a man and will die like one.

In the eve of Jefferson's execution Grant does not have the courage to see him die and goes to work and tells his students to pray at the time of the execution. Paul, a white deputy who befriended Jefferson in prison, comes to visit Grant after the execution and gives him Jefferson's diary. Paul offers Grant his friendship and he accepts.

4. Challenges of African-American citizen

In the middle of the 20th century, capital punishment has never been so firmly anchored in the US-American society and in the judiciary since the foundation of the USA. The challenges an African-American citizen had to face back in a time when it was both legal and endemic in the South to have racial segregation, a time when African-American citizen could barely hope for recognition of their humanity, a time where race and poverty affected people in the criminal justice system, in particular in capital punishment, barley changed. The major disadvantages of an African-American citizen are the racism and poverty, which still affect today's society. In the next chapters I will measure the predicament in the late 1940s until now.

4.1. Racism

The legacy of slavery and racist prejudices about the supposedly criminal character of African-American humans led to the inhuman living conditions. The major disadvantage that an African-American citizen had to face was therefore racism that was still present in the late 1940s. Even after the defeat of the Southern Confederacy in 1865 and the abolition of slavery[9] it was still an important goal of white planters to regain control of the African-American population. A number of Southern states enacted the so-called "Black Codes". These laws were aimed at former slaves by creating regulations and restrictions in their freedom from slavery and collusion their fundamental rights. These varied from state to state, but Black Codes meant basically limitations in the freedom of choosing their work or choice of a spouse and the prohibition of the statement or reduction of meaningfulness in court[10].

As example for a predicament for the African-American population and the importance of power for white planters was the court, which only consisted of all-white people. In order to better illustrate what period of time the novel was written in, is an example of the case of an African-American men who was accused of raping and murdering a white women. He was burned without a fair process by a mob in Missouri with a gruesome brutality[11]. In the case of Jefferson, the novel's wrongfully accused citizen, the white court allowed him a

---
9 Die Geschichte der Todesstrafe in Nordamerika – Von der Kolonialzeit bis zur Gegenwart, p.64
10 Hollis R. Lynch, "The Black Codes", URL: http://history-world.org/black_codes.htm [17.03.2015 ; 17:47]
11 Criminal Justice in the United States and Germany, p.33

trial but his attorney tried to make Jefferson look like an imbecile, not worth of electrocution:

> "Gentlemen of the jury, look at him. [...] Do you see a man sitting here? [...] I ask you, I implore, look carefully— [...] Look at the shape of this skull, this face as flat as the palm of my hand— look deeply into those eyes. Do you see a modicum of intelligence? Do you see anyone here who could plan a murder, a robbery, [...] can plan anything? [...] What you see here is a thing that acts on command. [...] That is what you see here [...]"[12]

This dehumanizing speech provides a gruesome picture of an African-American in the opinion of a white citizen. Studies also confirm the suspicion that in the course of time the decision of the exercise of capital punishment was still marked on racism[13]. In the time between 1930 and 1940 the proportion of African-American people among all legally executions in the United States rose from forty-eight percent to a "staggering" sixty percent and underlines that statement.

Beside Jefferson the narrator Grant Wiggins, an elementary school teacher, also has to face the discrimination of the white society. Although he is physically free, Grant created a mental prison because of his hatred for white humans. When Sheriff Guidry first had a conversation with Grant he says: "She doesn't, huh? [...] You're smart, [...] Maybe you're just a little to smart for your own good."[14] This only proved to Grant that he would be oppressed in this world because of his skin color. Due to the statement of Sheriff Guidry one can assume that the white civilization thought themselves to be the superior race and had less problems with the execution of African-American citizens. This thesis is also found in a realization that Grant makes while he got to know the time Jefferson's execution would take place. He says:

> How do people come up with a date and time to take life from another man? Who made them god? [...] Twelve white men say a black man must die, another white man sets the date and time without consulting one black person. Justice? [...] They sentence you to death [...] with no proof that

---

12 Ernest J. Gaines, *"A Lesson Before Dying"*, 2008 Ernst Klett Sprachen Stuttgart, p. 11
13 Richard C. Dieter, "*The Death Penalty in Black and White: Who Lives, Who Dies, Who Decides*", URL: http://www.deathpenaltyinfo.org/death-penalty-black-and-white-who-lives-who-dies-who-decides [27.02.2015 ; 23:08]
14 A Lesson Before Dying, p.46-47 l.10f.

you had anything at all to do with the crime [...]."[15]

Grant speaks thus one of the most important situations in the Criminal Justice System for African-Americans. Charles L. Black Jr., an American scholar of constitutional law professor, had the same opinion as the fictional character Grant. He had the opinion that "thought the justice of God may indeed ordain that some should die, the justice of man is altogether and always insufficient for saying who these may be"[16].

At one point, the teacher explains to his girlfriend how they are all trapped in a cycle of humiliation. She asks: "Will that circle ever be broken?" He answers, "It's up to Jefferson."[17] In the late 1940s the segregation based on race was regarded as a part of the daily life and the geography of the community Bayonne displayed exactly such a segregation of race with only a small and undesirable selection of establishments for black people[18]. This also stands as a symbol for the humiliation the African-American citizen had to suffer.

4.2. Poverty

Another disadvantage of African-American citizen is poverty. Humans tend to be quite judgmental when it comes to the subject of poverty. On one hand they belief that wealth comes to those who work for it which leads to the image that poor people have themselves to blame for their poverty. On the other hand those who are sympathetic for the poor blame the rich people for being to selfish and unfeeling to assist the poor.

In cases of capital punishment, the poor seldom find equal justice. Worldwide, the thing most people on death row have in common is their poverty, which suggests a link between poverty and capital punishment and a link between poverty and the ability to commit severe crime. It can be said that poor people have major disadvantages and in Jefferson's case it was the

---
15 A Lesson Before Dying, p.138 l.21f.
16 Criminal Justice in the United States and Germany, p.65
17 A Lesson Before Dying, p.146-147 l.32f.
18 A Lesson Before Dying, p.25 l.22f.

problem of not being able to effort a lawyer[19], which resulted in him getting an appointed lawyer from the court.

The problem of getting an appointed lawyer is that he can not be sure that he will be treated like every other client because the lawyer could be a racist and they often lacked the experience necessary for capital trials. Furthermore a court-appointed attorney was often overworked and underpaid and tended to capital punishment when the victim of a crime is white. The Supreme Court Justice Harry A. Blackmun did comment on the issues of a fair trial. He mentioned that even after twenty years and "despite the effort of the states and courts to devise legal formulas and procedural rules to meet this daunting challenge, the death penalty remains fraught with arbitrariness, discrimination, caprice, and mistake[20]." As an example of such a lawyer :

> A court-appointed defense lawyer's only reference to his client during the penalty phase of a Georgia capital case was: "You have got a little ole nigger man over there that doesn't weigh over 135 pounds. He is poor and he is broke. He's got an appointed lawyer [...] He is ignorant. I will venture to say he has an IQ of not over 80." The defendant was sentenced to death.[21]

When Jefferson stole the money of the dead storekeeper[22] it made him look guilty in the eye of the witness and sealed his fate to be executed. The likelyhood of him escaping the death row were nonexistent because there was no way that he would get a fair process. Even in the beginning of the 21th century it is still unlikely to offer equal justice when racial disparities plague the system[23].

---

19 A Lesson Before Dying, p.10 l.1-3
20 Harry A. Blackmun 1994 as the U.S. Supreme Court Justice, Amnesty International, URL: http://www.amnestyusa.org/our-work/issues/death-penalty/us-death-penalty-facts/death-penalty-and-arbitrariness [18.03.2015 ; 11:47]
21 Stephen B. Bright, "*Council for Poor: the Death Penalty Not for the Worst Crime but for the Worst Lawyer*", Yale Law Journal 103, no.7
22 A Lesson Before Dying, p.10 l.3-8
23 Senator Ross Feingold on Civil Rights as a Priority for the 108th Congress, Senat, 2003, URL: http://www.amnestyusa.org/our-work/issues/death-penalty/us-death-penalty-facts/death-penalty-and-race [28.02.2015 ; 23:32]

5. Comparison of the novel and reality

There are many controversies surrounding the use of capital punishment in the American criminal justice system, but while reading the novel "A Lesson Before Dying" I noticed that today's views on capital punishment can not be transferred to the former views in the society described in the book.

Jefferson's case took place in a time when African-Americans were not afforded equality not in society and especially in the criminal justice system. He was wrongfully accused and convicted by an all-white jury on death row for the robbery and murder of a storekeeper. It does make sense that this would look bad in the eyes of the court, for the legislation that was in place at the time of Jefferson's trial was different to today's, the trial was moreover motivated by racism and inequality[24]. A trial where a white jury would almost always find an African-American citizen guilty and sentenced to death for no better reason than the color of their skin.

The views of capital punishment in the book are unlike the views of today's civilization. The legislation in Louisiana in the late 1940s differs greatly from the legislation today. Executions are only carried out if the crime is a first degree murder and while the State has still not abandoned capital punishment they rarely use it anymore. Since the reintroduction on 2 July 1973, not more than 28 people were executed in total[25]. Furthermore the method of execution changed from electrocution to lethal injection since it seemed to be a more human form. While I am in no way saying that this type of justice is right, the number of executions sank and the State changed the law.

6. Survey results

In order to give an insight to today's acceptance of capital punishment I created a survey that aimed to aid my term paper in my research to the question to what extent capital punishment was accepted in the universe of the

---

24 Shelly Pinckney,*"Race and Civil Rights: the 30's and 40's"*, URL:
   http://depts.washington.edu/labhist/cpproject/pinckney.shtml [28.02.2015 ; 23:53]
25 Death Penalty Information Center, URL: http://www.deathpenaltyinfo.org/louisiana-1
   [01.03.2015 ; 00:11]

novel in contrast of the modern time. When creating this questionnaire I did allow the reader to answer with more than one option, but did not allow the reader to skip the question in order to get a full set of results.

The first bar charts (see appendix) aim to focus the attention on the results of the participants for any possible answer to the question if the exercise of capital punishment is right or wrong. As can be seen from the bar charts, the participants themselves are more likely to disagree about whether capital punishment should be abolished or if it depends on the crime a person has committed. With a number of 54% the result to the first question are that the exercise of capital punishment depends on the crime.

My second bar charts lay the attention on the results to the question if an African-American citizen in the late 1940s could prove their innocence in front of an all-white court. In this question the majority of participants agreed that it would not be possible for an African-American to prove their innocence in front of an all-white court with a number of 77%.

These results lead to the conclusion that, in frame of the participants, there will not be a total abolition of capital punishment in the near future. Nonetheless it concludes that there might come a time when humans will cease to execute other humans for a crime which might lead to the total abolition of capital punishment. In addition, based on the results of the second question, the majority of the participants hardly see a chance for an African-American to have a fair process.

7. Conclusion

It is safe to say that the views upon capital punishment greatly differ in history, thereby also in the universe of the novel and reality. On the one hand the execution of a human was an integral part of the human culture and more freely used for minor offenses, on the other hand the legislation for executions was reformed and is nowadays rarely used.

A white citizen in the late 1940s was more likely to sacrifice the life of an African-American because they grew up in a society with racial segregation. All children see their family as role models and are educated by them and if they notice their families aversion to African-American humans they will most certainly pick up that aspect. However, the changed connection in the novel between the white deputy Paul and the African-American teacher Grant Wiggins were one of the important points, for it ended with a start of a new friendship and made the reader hope for better times without prejudice and more tolerance. They showed that differences did not matter, only loyalty and a kind character.

In the mid-1960s the African-American population received at least a semblance of equal justice in the criminal justice system with the legislation of federal civil right[26]. And over time the opinions about foreigners and people with another skin color changed, essentially by Martin Luther Kings use and effective force in the Civil Rights Movement. African-American citizen have finally reached that racial segregation was repealed by law and the unrestricted suffrage was introduced for their population in the South of America[27]. The white population of America were educated to accept every human as an individual and understand the meaning of tolerance and thus the number of countries with capital punishment decreases.

The number of public supporters of capital punishment also increases and decreases over time because of the knowledge that it can not be administered fairly and accurately. If the number of supporters decreases to a new low point it might be the turning point and capital punishment will be abolished. When capital punishment was abolished in Germany in the late 1940s, only 21 percent of Germans favored abolition and 74 percent supported it[28], therefore it could function as a role model and support the United States in their effort to abolish it from their law.

So to close the question I claim that the citizen in the novel "A Lesson Before Dying" were more openly accepting capital punishment than the citizen of today's time. Even thought some people are still for capital punishment, there will come a time when the United States will cease to execute murderers and

---

26 Criminal Justice in the United States and Germany, p.28
27 Wikipedia, "*Martin Luther King Jr.*", URL: http://en.wikipedia.org/wiki/Martin_Luther_King_Jr. [17.03.2015 ; 18:20]
28 Criminal Justice in the United States and Germany, p.60

see the value of life[29].

8. List of references

Literature

Berg, Manfred / Kapsch, Stefan / Streng, Franz, *"Criminal Justice in the United States and Germany"*, Universitätsverlag WINTER Heidelberg, 2006

Gaines, Ernest J., *"A Lesson Before Dying"*, Ernst Klett Sprachen Stuttgart 2008

Martschukat, Jürgen, *"Die Geschichte der Todesstrafe in Nordamerika – Von der Kolonialzeit bis zur Gegenwart"*, Verlag C.H.Beck oHG, München 2002

Müller, Frank, *"Streitfall Todesstrafe"*, Patmos Verlag Düssedorf 1998

Internet

http://urbandreams.ousd.k12.ca.us/lessonplans/lessonbefore2/
http://www.un.org/en/documents/udhr/
http://www.deathpenaltyinfo.org/part-i-history-death-penalty
http://www.cliffsnotes.com/literature/l/a-lesson-before-dying/book-summary
http://www.deathpenaltyinfo.org/part-i-history-death-penalty#intro
http://history-world.org/black_codes.htm
http://www.deathpenaltyinfo.org/death-penalty-black-and-white-who-lives-who-dies-who-decides
http://www.amnestyusa.org/our-work/issues/death-penalty/us-death-penalty-facts/death-penalty-and-arbitrariness
http://www.amnestyusa.org/our-work/issues/death-penalty/us-death-penalty-facts/death-penalty-and-race
http://depts.washington.edu/labhist/cpproject/pinckney.shtml

---
29 Criminal Justice in the United States and Germany, p.71

http://www.deathpenaltyinfo.org/louisiana-1
http://en.wikipedia.org/wiki/Martin_Luther_King_Jr
http://www.shmoop.com/a-lesson-before-dying/
http://depts.washington.edu/labhist/cpproject/pinckney.shtml
http://video.law.yale.edu/media/introduction-and-death-penalty-history-s1a-2
http://drsjohnsoneducation.com/wp-content/uploads/2013/12/Poverty-Death-Penalty.pdf

9. Appendix

Death penalty - right or wrong?
Todesstrafe - Richtig oder Falsch?
13 out of 13 people answered this question

1 It depends on the crime / Es kommt auf das Verbrachen an	7 / 54%
2 I am against the death penalty / Ich bin gegen die Todesstrafe	5 / 38%
3 I am for the death penalty / Ich bin für die Todesstrafe	1 / 8%

Do you think an afro-american person in the 1940's could prove his innocence, even when the court only exists of white people?
Denkst du das ein Afro-Amerikaner im Jahr 1940 seine Unschuld beweisen könnte vor einer Jury voller hellhäutiger Menschen?
13 out of 13 people answered this question

1 No, that's impossible / Nein, das ist unmöglich	10 / 77%
2 It depends on the crime / Es kommt auf das Verbrechen an	2 / 15%
3 Yes, that is possible / Ja, das ist möglich	1 / 8%

YOUR KNOWLEDGE HAS VALUE

- We will publish your bachelor's and master's thesis, essays and papers

- Your own eBook and book - sold worldwide in all relevant shops

- Earn money with each sale

Upload your text at www.GRIN.com and publish for free